DW 597.7 RUS

## Animals Working Together

# Clown Fish and Sea Anemones Work Together

by Martha E. H. Rustad

**Consulting Editor:** Gail Saunders-Smith, PhD

**Consultant:** Jackie Gai, DVM
Zoo and Exotic Animal Consultation

CAPSTONE PRESS
a capstone imprint

Pebble Plus is published by Capstone Press,
151 Good Counsel Drive, P.O. Box 669, Mankato, Minnesota 56002.
www.capstonepub.com

Books published by Capstone Press are manufactured with paper
containing at least 10 percent post-consumer waste.

*Library of Congress Cataloging-in-Publication Data*
Rustad, Martha E. H. (Martha Elizabeth Hillman), 1975–
  Clown fish and sea anemones work together / by Martha E. H. Rustad.
    p. cm.—(Pebble plus. Animals working together)
  Includes bibliographical references and index.
  Summary: "Simple text and full-color photographs introduces the symbiotic relationship of clown fish and sea
anemones"—Provided by publisher.
  ISBN 978-1-4296-5297-1 (library binding)
  ISBN 978-1-4296-6198-0 (paperback)
  1. Anemonefishes—Ecology—Juvenile literature. 2. Sea anemones—Ecology—Juvenile literature. 3. Symbiosis—
Juvenile literature. I. Title. II. Series.
  QL638.P77R867 2011
  597'.7—dc22                                              2010025462

**Editorial Credits**
Erika L. Shores, editor; Bobbie Nuytten, designer; Svetlana Zhurkin, media researcher;
    Laura Manthe, production specialist

**Photo Credits**
Alamy/Stephen Frink Collection, 18–19
Brand X Pictures, 1
Digital Vision, 11
Dreamstime/Exploretimor, cover, 20–21; Jose Manuel Gelpi Diaz, 4–5; Olga Khoroshunova, 12–13
Photodisc, 6–7
Shutterstock/Rich Carey, 15; Tatiana Belova, 9; Tyler Fox, 16–17

## Note to Parents and Teachers

The Animals Working Together series supports national science standards related to biology.
This book describes and illustrates the relationship between clown fish and sea anemones. The
images support early readers in understanding the text. The repetition of words and phrases
helps early readers learn new words. This book also introduces early readers to subject-specific
vocabulary words, which are defined in the Glossary section. Early readers may need assistance
to read some words and to use the Table of Contents, Glossary, Read More, Internet Sites, and
Index sections of the book.

Printed in the United States of America in North Mankato, Minnesota.
092010
005933CGS11

# Table of Contents

# Symbiosis

A clown fish swims near a coral reef. Sea anemone tentacles wiggle nearby. The fish darts into the stinging tentacles. Is the fish in danger?

The clown fish is safe.

Stings from sea anemones

do not hurt clown fish.

Slimy mucus covers clown fish

scales and protects it from stings.

Sea anemones and clown fish are animal partners. Each helps the other find food, shelter, and safety. This relationship is called symbiosis.

# Sea Anemones Help Clown Fish

Clown fish stay safe

in sea anemones.

Clown fish hide from predators

in anemone tentacles.

# Clown Fish Help Sea Anemones

Sea anemones attach to reefs.

Their stinging tentacles wait

for fish, shrimp, and other prey.

Clown fish lure prey to
sea anemones. Clown fish
swim through the tentacles.
Other fish think the sea anemone
is safe and get stung.

Clown fish eat parasites and leftover food scraps on anemones. Clown fish get food, and the anemones stay clean and healthy.

Predators such as butterfly fish

try to eat anemones.

Clown fish click their teeth

to scare away predators.

# Teamwork

On a busy coral reef,
clown fish and sea anemones
are a team. Symbiosis keeps
both animals healthy and safe.

# Glossary

**coral reef**—an area of coral skeletons and rocks in shallow ocean water

**lure**—to try to get something to come closer

**mucus**—a slimy, thick liquid

**parasite**—a small organism that lives on or inside an animal or person; parasites sometimes hurt the animal it lives on or inside

**scale**—one of the small, thin plates that covers the bodies of fish

**sting**—to hurt with a poisoned tip; sea anemones sting prey with their tentacles

**symbiosis**—a relationship between two different kinds of animals; the animals live together to help each other find food, shelter, or safety

**tentacle**—a long, flexible arm of an animal; sea anemones sting prey with their tentacles

# Read More

**Levy, Janey.** *Discovering Coral Reefs.* World Habitats. New York : Rosen Pub. Group's PowerKids Press, 2008.

**Rake, Jody Sullivan.** *Sea Anemones.* Under the Sea. Mankato, Minn.: Capstone Press, 2006.

**Silverman, Buffy.** *You Scratch My Back.* Raintree Fusion. Chicago: Raintree, 2008.

# Internet Sites

FactHound offers a safe, fun way to find Internet sites related to this book. All of the sites on FactHound have been researched by our staff.

Here's all you do:

Visit *www.facthound.com*

Type in this code: 9781429652971

Super-cool stuff! Check out projects, games and lots more at **www.capstonekids.com**

# Index

Word Count: 185
Grade: 1
Early-Intervention Level: 17